WELCOME TO POLAND

COUNTRIES OF THE WORLD

Poland

by Jennifer Joline Anderson

BLASTOFF! READERS 2

BLASTOFF! READERS, AN IMPRINT OF BELLWETHER MEDIA BY FLUTTERBEE

Blastoff! Readers are carefully developed by literacy experts to build reading stamina and move students toward fluency by combining standards-based content with developmentally appropriate text.

LEVELS

Level 1 provides the most support through repetition of high-frequency words, light text, predictable sentence patterns, and strong visual support.

Level 2 offers early readers a bit more challenge through varied sentences, increased text load, and text-supportive special features.

Level 3 advances early-fluent readers toward fluency through increased text load, less reliance on photos, advancing concepts, longer sentences, and more complex special features.

★ **Blastoff! Universe**

Reading Level

Blastoff! Beginners — Grade K

Blastoff! Readers — Grades 1–3

Blastoff! Discovery — Grade 4

This edition first published in 2027 by Bellwether Media, Inc.

For information regarding permission, write to Bellwether Media, Inc., Attention: Permissions Department, 3500 American Blvd W, Suite 150, Bloomington, MN 55431.

Library of Congress Cataloging-in-Publication Data is available at www.loc.gov or upon request from the publisher.

ISBN: 9798898800482 (hardcover)
ISBN: 9798898801724 (ebook)

Editor: Betsy Rathburn Designer: Laura Sowers

Printed in the United States of America, North Mankato, MN.

Table of Contents

All About Poland

Warsaw

Poland is a large country in Central Europe. Its capital is Warsaw.

Poland has a long history. It is known for beautiful forests and colorful cities.

Land and Animals

Most of Poland is flat. Forests cover large areas of the country.

Mountains rise in the south. The Baltic Sea touches the north coast. It has sandy beaches.

Baltic Sea

Białowieża Forest

Size: 548 square miles (1,419 square kilometers)

Famous For: a very old, large forest in eastern Poland

Poland is warm in the summer.
In the winter, it is cold and snowy.

The coast is mild. The mountains are cooler.

White-tailed eagles fly over **plains**. Chamois climb high peaks. Shy porpoises swim near the coast.

European bison

Animals of Poland

white-tailed eagle

chamois

brown bear

European bison

Wolves, bears, and squirrels live in forests. Bison **roam** free.

Life in Poland

Most Poles live in cities. Warsaw is the biggest. It has around 2 million people.

Polish is the main language. Most people are **Roman Catholic**.

English: Hello
Polish: Cześć
(CHE-sht)

Horseback riding is a favorite activity. **Foraging** is also common. The most popular sport is soccer.

The mazurka is a Polish **folk dance**. It is lively and fast!

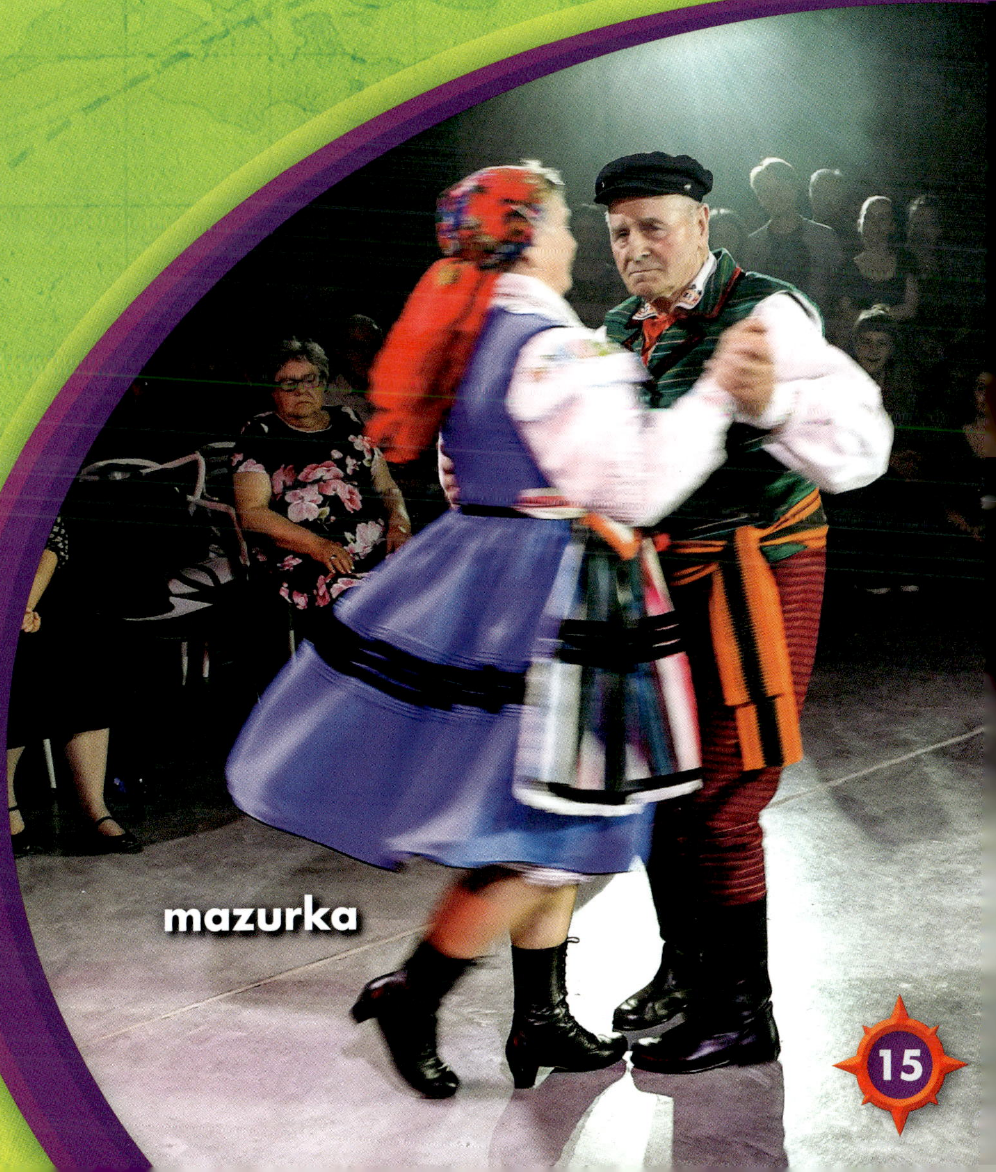

Kielbasa is a Polish sausage. Pierogi are dumplings filled with meat, potatoes, and cheese.

Polish Foods

kielbasa

pierogi

bigos

pączki

Bigos is a hearty stew. *Pączki* are fried donuts filled with jam.

Easter and Christmas are important holidays. For Easter, families bring baskets of food to church to be **blessed**.

May 3 is Constitution Day. People wave Polish flags. They **celebrate** Polish **culture**.

Constitution Day

blessing
Easter baskets

Poland Facts

Size:
120,728 square miles
(312,685 square kilometers)

Population:
38,746,310 (2024)

National Holiday:
Constitution Day (May 3)

Main Language:
Polish

Capital City:
Warsaw

Famous Face

Name: Iga Swíatek

Famous For: professional tennis player

Religions

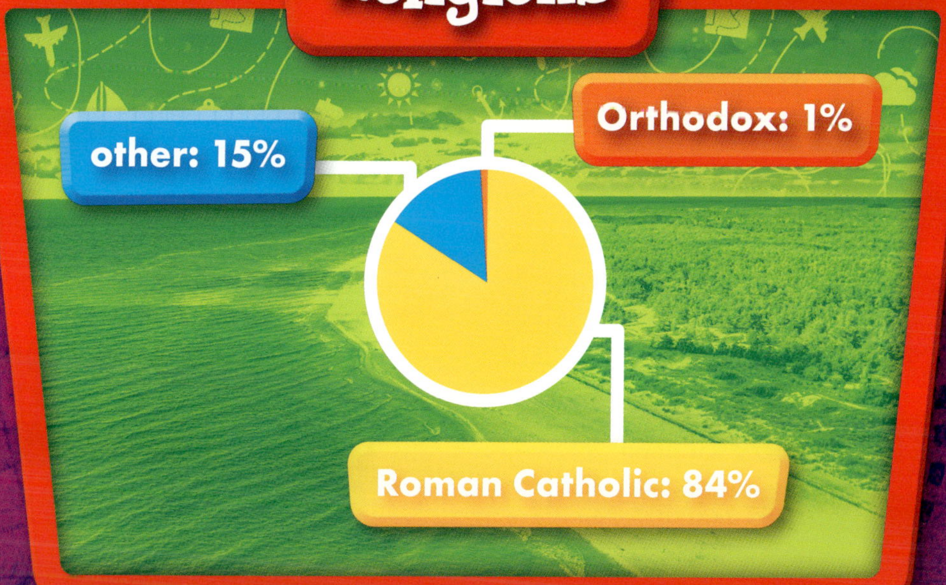

Top Landmarks

Auschwitz-Birkenau State Museum

Wawel Royal Castle

Wieliczka Salt Mine

Glossary

blessed—made holy

celebrate—to do something special or fun for an event, occasion, or holiday

culture—the beliefs, arts, and ways of life in a place or society

folk dance—a traditional dance of the people in a country or region

foraging—searching the outdoors for plants, mushrooms, and other things that can be eaten

plains—large areas of flat land

roam—to travel freely over an area

Roman Catholic—belonging to or related to the Christian church that is lead by the pope

To Learn More

AT THE LIBRARY

Heale, Jay. *Poland*. Buffalo, N.Y.: Cavendish Square Publishing, 2025.

Mather, Charis. *A Visit to Poland*. Minneapolis, Minn.: Bearport Publishing, 2024.

Spanier, Kristine. *Poland*. Minneapolis, Minn.: Jump!, 2021.

ON THE WEB

FACTSURFER

Factsurfer.com gives you a safe, fun way to find more information.

1. Go to www.factsurfer.com.
2. Enter "Poland" into the search box and click .
3. Select your book cover to see a list of related content.

Index

The images in this book are reproduced through the courtesy of: Stepniak, front cover; Piotr Krzeslak, front cover, p. 11 (brown bear, European bison); WDnet Studio, p. 3; fotorince, pp. 4-5; shaiith, p. 6; Grzegorz Lenkiewicz, pp. 6-7; Aneta, pp. 8-9; Photocreo Bednarek, p. 9; WildMedia, pp. 10-11; henk bogaard, p. 11 (white-tailed eagle); TTstudio, p. 11 (chamois); Patryk Kosmider, p. 12; Anastasiia Sienotova/ Westend61/ SuperStock, pp. 12-13; pikselstock, p. 14; Pawel Kazmierczak, pp. 14-15; JANEK SKARZYNSKI/ Getty Images, p. 15; Gravika, p. 16 (kielbasa); Brent Hofacker, p. 16 (pierogi); HLPhoto, p. 16 (*bigos*); czarny_bez, p. 16 (*pączki*); RomanBabakin, p. 17; Avalon_Studio, p. 18; Adam Bartosik, pp. 18-19; adidas4747, p. 20 (flag); Hameltion/ Wikipedia, p. 20 (Iga Świątek); CL-Medien, p. 21 (Auschwitz-Birkenau State Museum); itph, p. 21 (Wawel Royal Castle); Diego Grandi, p. 21 (Wieliczka Salt Mine); losonsky, p. 20.